FLUTE (PICCOLO)

TRIOS FOR ALL

arranged by KENNETH HENDERSON and ALBERT STOUTAMIRE

CONTENTS

INSTRUMENTATION

V 1392 Flute (Piccolo)
V 1393 B♭ Clarinet (Bass Clarinet)
V 1394 B♭ Cornet
V 1395 E♭ Alto Saxophone (E♭ Baritone Saxophone)
    (E♭ Clarinet) (E♭ Alto Clarinet)
V 1396 F Horn

V1397 Trombone (Baritone B. C.)
    (Bassoon) (Tuba)
V1398 Baritone T. C. (B♭ Tenor Saxophone)
V1399 Violin
V1400 Viola
V1401 Cello & Bass

V1402 Piano-Conductor
(Oboe-Mallet Instrument)
(Harp-Guitar)

Pro Vol 1392

D1279231

FOREWORD

A variety of combinations of instruments can play trios with these books. With the exception of the basses, any three like instruments such as three flutes, three clarinets, three cornets, three trombones, three bassoons, and so on can play together in three part harmony. Numerous dissimilar instruments such as violin, trumpet, and tuba also may perform all of the trios in these books. Basses must play the bottom line only, but the music is arranged so that they have the melody from time to time.

Any number of instrumentalists may play together in three part harmony. Thus, directors can rehearse the music with large ensembles and assign trios of players or groups of players to practice and perform together.

This set of books meets the needs of friends and neighbors who wish to play together for festivals, concerts, or just for fun, whether or not their instruments are traditional combinations. The pieces also make excellent material for auditions and sight-reading.

FEATURES

The material covers a wide range of styles and music by composers from Baroque through contemporary eras.

The trios range in difficulty from grades I through IV.

The pages are laid out in an identical manner in each book so that performers can quickly locate a point for discussion or rehearsal. No page turning is required when playing.

SUGGESTIONS

When high sounding instruments and a low sounding instrument (violin, trumpet, and tuba for example) play a trio, the high instruments play the upper lines while the low instrument plays the bottom line. Bass clarinets, tuba and contrabass instruments always play the bottom line only.

Interesting effects can be obtained by combining several trios of instruments. Three violins may play trios simultaneously with three cellos. Three flutes, three clarinets, and three bassoons make an interesting triple trio group. Three cornets and three trombones blend well as a double trio. Also, several like instruments (horns for example) can play the top part in unison while several other like instruments (trombones for example) play the second part and basses play their part (the third line).

RIGADOON

Animato

HENRY PURCELL

IVAN SINGS

ARAM KHACHATURIAN

ANDANTE

W. A. MOZART

THEME
(from Symphony No. 1)

JOHANNES BRAHMS

Allegro

HUNTER'S SONG

L. VAN BEETHOVEN

PASSEPIED

GEORG PHILLIP TELLEMANN

MENUET

G. F. HANDEL

Allegro grazioso

ANDANTE GRAZIOSO

FRANZ JOSEF HAYDN

Andante grazioso

LITTLE MARCH

DMITRI SHOSTAKOVICH

SOLDIERS MARCH

Tempo di marcia

ROBERT SCHUMANN

BALLET ANGLOIS

JOHANN K. F. FISCHER

DIRGE

BÉLA BARTÓK

MARCH

S. PROKOFIEV

WALTZ

Allegro moderato

EDVARD GRIEG

19

Pro Vol 1392

DANCE

DMITRI KABALEVSKY

KAMARINSKAIA

Allegro vivo

P. I. TSCHAIKOWSKY

LARGHETTO

IGOR STRAVINSKY

INSTRUMENTAL ENSEMBLES FOR ALL
DUETS FOR ALL • TRIOS FOR ALL • CLASSICAL QUARTETS FOR ALL
by Albert Stoutamire and Kenneth Henderson

Any combination and any number of instruments can play together in harmony. Woodwinds, brass, strings and mallet percussion (even snare drum in **DUETS FOR ALL**) can have fun playing in like-instrument or mixed-instrument ensembles.

The material covers a wide range of styles and music by composers from Baroque through contemporary eras.

DUETS FOR ALL and **TRIOS FOR ALL** range in difficulty from grades I through IV. **QUARTETS FOR ALL** range in difficulty from grades I through III.

The pages are laid out in an identical manner in each book so that all performers can quickly locate a point for discussion or rehearsal. No page turns are required when playing.

This set of books will meet the needs of classmates, friends, family and neighbors who want to play together for festivals, concerts or just for fun. They are also excellent for learning ensemble playing, auditions and sight reading.

DUETS FOR ALL • TRIOS FOR ALL • QUARTETS FOR ALL
fit your every need!

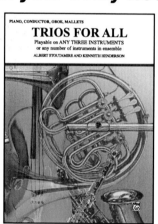

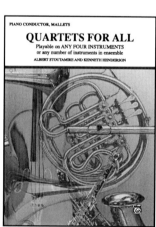

DUETS FOR ALL
Stoutamire and Henderson

(PROBK01337) **Piano Conductor, Mallets**
(PROBK01324) **Flute, Piccolo**
(PROBK01325) **Oboe, Guitar**
(PROBK01326) **B♭ Clarinet, Bass Clarinet**
(PROBK01327) **E♭ Saxes, E♭ Clarinets**
(PROBK01328) **Tenor Saxophone**
(PROBK01329) **Cornet, Baritone T.C.**
(PROBK01330) **F Horn**
(PROBK01331) **Trombone, Baritone, Bassoon**
(PROBK01332) **Tuba**
(PROBK01333) **Snare Drum**
(PROBK01334) **Violin**
(PROBK01335) **Viola**
(PROBK01336) **Cello & Bass**

TRIOS FOR ALL
Stoutamire and Henderson

(PROBK01402) **Piano, Conductor, Oboe, Mallets**
(PROBK01392) **Flute, Piccolo**
(PROBK01393) **B♭ Clarinet, Bass Clarinet**
(PROBK01394) **Cornet**
(PROBK01395) **E♭ Saxes, E♭ Clarinets**
(PROBK01396) **F Horn**
(PROBK01397) **Trombone, Baritone B.C., Bassoon, Tuba**
(PROBK01398) **Baritone T.C.**
(PROBK01399) **Violin**
(PROBK01400) **Viola**
(PROBK01401) **Cello, Bass**

QUARTETS FOR ALL
Stoutamire and Henderson

(PROBK01435) **Piano Conductor, Mallets**
(PROBK01427) **C Treble Instruments**
(PROBK01428) **B♭ Treble Instruments**
(PROBK01429) **E♭ Treble Instruments**
(PROBK01430) **F Instruments**
(PROBK01431) **Bass Clef Instruments**
(PROBK01432) **Violin**
(PROBK01433) **Viola**
(PROBK01434) **Cello, Bass**

Belwin

Alfred
alfred.com

ISBN-10: 0-7692-5581-7
ISBN-13: 978-0-7692-5581-1

9 780769 255811

PROBK01392 $7.99

0 29156 14786 5

ISBN 0-7692-5581-7

W8-BNE-116